Happy Parenting Happy Children

Happy Parenting Happy Children

9 *Essential Guidelines for Parents and Helping Professionals*

Mira Walker M.A.
Licensed Marriage and Family Therapist

Abundant Light Publishing
Kauai, Hawaii

HAPPY PARENTING HAPPY CHILDREN
  HappyParentingHappyChildren.com
  MiraWalker.com

Published by Abundant Light Publishing
  Kauai, Hawaii

ISBN: 978-0-9979715-0-7

Printed in the United States of America

Cover and book design by
Judah Freed, HokuHouse.com

Front cover photo by Sarah Walker
Back cover photo by Candace Freeland

Dedication

With a smile in my heart, I honor the
caregivers of the world's children.
You are creating the future.
All is possible! Blessings Be!

Table of Contents

Preface

For almost 30 years, my work as a licensed Marriage Family Therapist has focused on helping families and children. I assist co-parents, separated parents and single parents.

I've helped many families through my private practice, as a contractor for community agencies, and by providing consulting services for active-duty military families in the USA and in Europe. These varied yet focused experiences have given me the ability and insight to see family patterns that foster happy parenting and happy children. I offer the following nine parenting guidelines, with compassion and gratitude for all the adults caring for the world's children.

If you are a parent reading this, then you already believe there is a way to create a "happy parenting, happy children" experience. Believing this is possible, that you really can have a more joyful and harmonious family life, is what it takes for it to happen. The nine essential guidelines here are designed to support your journey along the way to that goal.

If you are a helping professional working with families, these essential guidelines can reinforce the positive outcome you strive for in your work. Sharing these guidelines with families that come to you for guidance (in their steps along the path) can build a strong foundation for enhancing the *happy parenting, happy children* experience.

By sharing and condensing my life's work into these nine guidelines, I hope to add to the happiness, peace and joy of the parents and children of the world. *May it be so!* Blessings Be.

Acknowledgements

The book owes its inspiration and inception to the families who have come to me for professional guidance over a period of 30 years.

Each adult and child has been my teacher, enriching my life in his or her own unique way. The families who worked and played with me are the people who actually wrote this book, in a way. These many families, in varied stages of life, had may issues. I supported intact families, separated families, and single-parent families, as well as multi-generational families.

I facilitated the process, yet the dedication to better their family life forms the basis of how this book came into being. I feel that it's important to share our collaboration with a wider audience of parents and family professionals. So, I feel much gratitude to those who are unnamed here but are very present in the writing.

I also acknowledge Judah Freed, a published author, mentor, coach, and friend. Without all his professional offerings to writers in our community, this book would still be an unfinished manuscript on my computer. His perseverance and devotion to stay in integrity and keep positive, even during challenging times, provided me with a role model that will be with me in all aspects of my life.

Thank You!
Mira Walker, MFT

Happy
Parenting
Happy
Children

INTRODUCTION

The Overall Guidelines: Love, Compassion, Gratitude

R emembering the amazing miracle of life, applying the nine guidelines here with love, compassion and gratitude, can be your path to a *happy parenting, happy children* experience. The guidelines are pointers; they are not rules.

Love, as it relates to being a parent, means being gentle with yourself. Love means giving yourself the room to be innately who you are as you support the unique nature of a child to grow into his or her creativity and empowerment. It's the greatest opportunity to *be in love*. It's also the greatest opportunity to not just *be* in love, but to

3

see that love, children and parenting take many forms. Love and the way you express love, grows into a larger understanding of how to find the joy of a *happy parenting, happy children* experience.

Love also means doing the best you can each moment, not falling into a false concept that you need to do it right. There is no right. There is only striving to be present in each situation, staying conscious of the miracle of each human being.

When there is a challenging situation, take a breath and try to envision a child's process from conception to birth. Then take two more breaths. This process will allow consciousness to unfold and guide you back to the person you truly are, and to be the parent you want to be with a smile in your heart.

Love means remembering that being a parent isn't always easy. It's a challenging and rewarding job that continues to change and grow as you, the parent, change and grow along with the child. It offers parents an opportunity to stretch beyond what they could have imagined in all realms: emotional, physical, mental and spiritual. It lets you open your heart to express love and receive love in unimaginable ways.

Introduction

The word *compassion* means compassion for yourself and the children. Compassion for yourself is remembering that you are human, not a superhuman being. Compassion allows you to see the areas that you want to do differently without the negative self-talk that may want to engage you. It's hearing the internal dialog and focusing on a realization that you are hearing the internal dialog, and meanwhile feeling compassion for yourself. Hearing the internal dialog with compassion allows the dialog to change.

Compassion means compassion for yourself and for the children.

Compassion for children is remembering that each moment is a tremendous learning moment. Children are often in the present moment and their experience of what is important can be very different from that of an adult. They imitate, they forget, they sense the world from a perspective of self and their limited understanding.

Remember to call up compassion in the midst of being challenged when a child brings up anger or frustration in you. Bringing in compassion is the biggest step towards being compassionate.

The word *gratitude* means that you touch that place deep within you that sees gratitude in the opportunity to be a guiding presence in a child's positive development. Gratitude within parenting also means that when you become aware you want to change your reaction or way of relating to your child, you wrap that awareness with gratitude. Being conscious and aware that you want to change allows the change to happen. Gratitude is allowing into your heart the knowing that being a parent gives you the opportunity to make a lasting contribution to the future of humanity.

Gratitude for becoming conscious and aware that you want to change allows the change to happen.

The nine guidelines are applicable for dual parents, single parents and separated parents. Sections in each guideline, if appropriate, modify or expand the guideline to fit the needs of parents in a given population. Please be sure to read the full guideline before you read a section for single or separated parents. Each guideline builds on the previous one. Each guideline is a pointer you can adapt to your unique situation.

Introduction

The word *parent* is used to encompass all the unique combinations used to name the primary caregivers of the children. This can mean any combination of adults. The guidelines also apply to extended family members and can extend to professional primary caregivers. The guidelines can be applied if children receive care outside the home, such as in situations where parents are working for extended hours or time periods.

> **The word parent is used to encompass all the unique combinations to name the primary caregivers of the children.**

The guidelines can open up new possibilities as they shift old thought patterns that have been blocking your creative energy. They can make parenting more fun and exciting. It's important to follow your intuition, to get more information, and to experiment with these concepts.

GUIDELINE 1

Parents Need to Be Nurtured

When you fly in an airplane, the safety guidelines always emphasize that if the oxygen mask is dropping down for you to use ALWAYS put the mask on the adult before you put it on the child.

In order to give love and caring to a child, a parent's needs are of major importance. An empty pitcher of water cannot give water. Finding ways to be nurtured is not a selfish act. It's an act of loving yourself as you recognize and take care of yourself so that you can truly be present and care for and love others.

A parent who has not stopped to fill their pitcher of patience, love, kindness, caring, understanding, cleaning-up after, having compassion for, being the decision maker, running the family logistics, etc., becomes an empty pitcher. It's of major importance to become conscious before the pitcher is getting to empty, so that you can fill it up and be the parent you want to be.

It's essential that you find unique ways to care for yourself in the routine of your daily life patterns. Here are a few examples of finding ways to create self-care and nurturing into your daily life:

• Getting up earlier, or going to bed later, to give yourself the time for that warm bath, or to read a chapter in the inspiring or fantasy book (not the parenting book).

• Watch at least part of a great movie or find a spot to light a candle so you can sit quietly.

• Listen to calming music, or get a massage.

• Take a walk or find time to be with a friend. It could be finding a caregiver or a trade person to go away for a few hours, for a half a day, a full day, a weekend, or even a week.

• Spend time connecting with the inner dialog that says, "If I only had the time to do (blank), I'd feel better and have more energy."

Then find a way to fulfill that need. It's not just for the parent that this guideline exists. As the parent benefits, so will the children.

If you are a two-parent family It's also important to nurture your relationship. It's essential to recognize that nurturing the relationship ultimately nurtures the family environment for a *happy parenting, happy children* experience.

Just as one person needs to become conscious of how they feel nurtured, the relationship needs call to be recognized as they are also of primary importance. Plan in advance to go on dates, have dinners together, watch an adult movie or just take the time for an adult only walk. However it will work in your adult relationship the important aspect is that you take the time to be together in a relaxed way. Giving your relationship the importance it deserves is invaluable for the family.

It's essential that you find unique ways to care for yourself in the routine of your daily life patterns.

Single Parents:

It may be more difficult for you to find time for self-care and self-nurturing. This means it's even more important that you find ways to find respite from your parenting responsibilities.

Finding time to have "adult" activities in your life is a primary necessity when you are a single parent. Of course, being a parent is a very important part of your life, but do not give up the adult activities that you enjoy. Stepping away from the parental role and identity, even if it's just for a quiet and warm bath, can rejuvenate you and help you be present for children in a healthy, joyful way.

Sometimes single parents think they need to do more because they are a one-adult family. If a single parent gives all of their energy to the children, they can come to feel isolated and exhausted. A single parent can find support from other single parents. Support can be found by reaching out to parenting groups, school functions and children events. You may be the single adult in your family, but you can join with others in similar situations to share time and be nurtured.

Separated Parents:

If you take turns caring for the children, use opportunities when you don't have the children to consciously find an adult activity to provide self-care and nurturing. Set something up in advance and follow through with it. It can be special time for you. Recognize it's essential. If you are a separated and single parent be sure to read the single parent section.

GUIDELINE 2

Children Think Differently Than Adults

When we are learning to read we begin with the ABCs. After we learn to read, we rarely think of the ABCs, we just read. Everyone knows that children are not little adults, but most often we forget the ABCs of why children are different than adults.

When we forget the differences between a child's cognitive abilities and an adult's ability, both the parents and the children can become frustrated and feel incompetent.

Remembering to apply this understanding of the child's cognitive development will allow you to build a firm foundation for the building blocks that form the core of happy parenting, happy children.

Infants and children comprehend and see the world differently then their adult caregivers. They are often focused on the present moment without thinking about past and future. Children's brains and cognitive abilities are in rapid growth patterns. It's easy to remember this when the child is an infant.

However, as the infant becomes a toddler and develops language skills and the ability to mimic older children or an adult, this fact becomes harder to remember. It's at this point in a child's development that parents often have cognitive expectations from their child, which are not possible according to the studies of children's cognitive development and ability.

Children cannot physiologically think like adults by using abstract thinking, abstract reasoning or abstract logical thinking. They cannot begin to think like adults until they are preteens. Children's brains continue to grow as they develop towards adulthood. The physiological ability to do abstract thinking and think like an adult does not start to come to completion until children are between the ages of 11 and 14.

Just as each child matures physically in a unique time line, there are developmental milestones in thinking that also develop. This biological development of the brain is why we see preteens and teenagers trying to find themselves. "Finding yourself" is an abstract concept. Understanding that your parents are people with their own emotional lives, concerns, difficulties and responsibilities, other then caring for you, are abstract concepts.

Although children do not have brains that are physiologically developed to do abstract thinking, they can act like they have that ability. Young children can repeat what they hear and then repeat in a context that seems like they are able to understand abstraction. The reality of understanding and integrating knowledge is still very much in the process of developing.

An Example:
Children repeat what they have been told about death and it does seem they understand. A child can repeat that an animal has died and is now in the spirit world. Integrating and

understanding the complexity of this abstract concept is usually not possible until this area of the brain is more fully formed. The child who can say that something or someone is dead and that they are in the spirit world, will often in play wake up that "dead" one and have them be reborn.

The physiological ability to do abstract thinking and "think like an adult" does not start to come to completion until children are between the ages of 11 and 14.

It's common for many adults to still ponder the concept of dying. Yet the child's version is concrete and often means the dead are simply not visible right now.

According to cognitive developmental theories, which describe how children's ways of thinking develops, there are ages and stages of development. Swiss psychologist Jean Piaget created the most well-known and accepted cognitive development stage theory. Piaget's theory has basic four stages: (1) Sensorimotor, (2) Preoperational, (3) Concrete Operational, and (4) Formal Operational.

During the *sensorimotor* stage, which often lasts approximately until around age two, children are beginning to learn how to learn many things. They are learning to use their bodies. The beginning of language develops in accordance with their thoughts. This learning involves the five senses, and it's categorized by crawling, walking, being able to point at things, and beginning to use language.

The next stage Piaget outlined is called the *preoperational* stage, which develops from ages two though seven. During this stage we see children develop the ability to use mental symbols to understand and interact with the world. They continue to master language skills. It's often at this stage we see children have the ability to engage in pretend play. At this time, adults may begin to forget that the child's abstract ability is not fully developed. Breakthroughs to more advanced levels of thinking are not yet complete.

Piaget called the third stage the *concrete operational* stage. This stage continues from ages seven to around 11. In this developmental stage, we see children gain the ability to think more logically. They can solve problems and better organize information. At this stage, we sometimes think children can "think like adults." However, they remain mostly limited to cognition that is only concrete and not abstract because at this stage the capability for abstract thought is not yet fully developed. Children at this stage can solve concrete problems, not abstract ones.

An Example:

The family went for a walk and the meat for dinner was left where the dog could see it and reach it. When the family comes home and goes into the kitchen, they see that the meat is no longer where they left it. The family dog is sitting in the kitchen close to where the meat had been and he is licking his lips. A child at this stage of development could come up with the concept that the dog ate the meat. All the elements in this example are concrete and do not use abstract cognitive maturation.

The last stage that Piaget formulated is called *formal operational* stage, and spans the age 11 and onward. In this stage, adolescents are developing the ability to think more abstractly. They can think symbolically and more rationally and will be able to solve problems that are not only of a concrete nature. It's at this stage that they do not need visual or tactile information to formulate answers to abstract ideas. They may start to self reflect and ask themselves questions related to the development of their abstract thinking ability. "Who am I separate from my parents? What do I believe in? How can I be more popular, attractive or different from my peers?"

At this stage of development, a child begins to have the ability to comprehend that their parent actually has a real life besides being a parent. The ability of a child to understand that an adult has his or her own feelings, problems, joys and needs is a welcome development for the parents. It's often hard to remember that this ability of abstract thinking does not develop until somewhere between the ages of 11 and 14.

Recent studies also formulate that in some people, abstract ability continues to develop throughout their lives. This is thought to be true for those people capable of exploring complicated and abstract ideas. Theoretical scientists, mathematicians, astrophysicists and others are examples of having expanded abstract thinking abilities.

GUIDELINE 3

Emotional Stability: Knowing Your Parents Will Take Care of You

Since children's brains are still developing and are unable to think like adults, they need adults to care and provide for them. Even the most willful child will feel insecure if an adult does not give the guidance, the support, and the material needs for them to develop.

Children often will find ways to test parents so they can be sure that their parents are able to care for them. When they are sure that their parents are willing and able to care for them, the child will relax and just be a child. They will no longer need to act like an adult. This will bring clarity to the situation.

Have you ever seen truck drivers pull into a gas station to check their tires? After they fill the gas tank, they then go to each tire to check its condition. They kick the tires to be sure they are strong. When drivers are confident the tires can do the job, then drivers get back in the cab and pay full attention to driving. They are now calm and secure that they have cared for their truck.

Children may do a very similar thing. They "kick" at the parental structure to see if the parents are able to care for them. When they find holes in the structure, they push harder because insecurity arises, so they want to find out if they need to be the one in control.

Parents understand that it's their job to take care of their children. Children feel secure when they receive a clear message that their parents will do their job to take care of them. When children feel insecure and wonder if the parents are able to take care of them, they try to move into the adult role. A child who tries to move into the adult structure will bargain, negotiate endlessly, and up the ante to get the parent to do their job.

Children really lack the abstract abilities to make adult decisions. Children need adults to keep them healthy, safe and protected. They feel secure when they know the parents will listen, evaluate and then make adult decisions on how best to do their parent job. The more a child understands that the parents are doing their job in a loving and caring way, the more the child can relax and be a happy child.

> **Children feel secure when they receive a clear message that their parents will do their "job" to take care of them.**

Here are some examples of what parents might say to their children so they can feel fully secure that the adults are taking care of them.

"My job as your parent is to take care of you. I hear that you want only your dessert, but it's my job to be sure you are healthy and eat good food. Dessert is available *after* you eat a good meal."

Alternatively: "I heard what you want to do, but it's my job as your parent to keep you safe.

I have decided that it's not a safe thing to do. You can ride your bike here, but not there."

Using the truck driver metaphor, a child may kick at the decision to see how much power they have to make a hole in the adult structure. There will be many opportunities to demonstrate for your children that it's because you love them that you make the decisions that help them grow, be safe, and be happy. When children kick at the parental structure and find strong loving parents, they will stop kicking to find the holes.

GUIDELINE 4

Building The Parental Structure

The parents who present their care-giving from a perspective of "we" offer the child a clear understanding that there are two or more people working together to do the parenting job. If not in a two-parent family, the other "parent" may be an extended family member, friend or primary caregiver.

Parents do not have to pretend that they always agree. The message to the children can be that disagreement happens and the parents will work out a solution. One of the holes that sometimes appears in a two-parent caregiver family occurs when the parents are easily split and divided in the decision-making process of how best to care for their child.

Many parents can provide a united front on the big parenting decisions. In the everyday caring and decision-making process, children often become aware that their parents are not united. When children realize their parents disagree in the everyday job of caring for them,

> When children realize that their parents disagree in the everyday job of caring for them a hole appears in the parenting structure.

a hole appears in the parenting structure. Insecurity arises if children realize that adults are in conflict about their job as the parents and how to care for the child.

Each child's emotional makeup is quite unique but some patterns occur when children feel insecure about their parents' united ability to care for them. One behavior that often arises if children are insecure is the "split and divide" exploration. This usually takes the form of one parent being perceived as the "good" parent and the other the "not so good," or in children's mind as the "bad" parent. This occurs when the parents often are in conflict of how to resolve everyday issues that can escalate into parental disharmony and relationship difficulties.

A child's desire to get what they want will lead them to check out the abilities of parents to see if the parents can be split and divided. It's important that the child does not perceive that they have the ability to make this good parent/bad parent hole in the family structure. It's normal for parents to disagree on decisions related to their children.

The parents can agree to disagree and still remain in the adult structure by working out their disagreement when the children are not present. Parents can acknowledge that they have a different opinion on the issue by letting the children know that they will discuss the matter and inform them of the "we" decision.

Two Examples:

1. One parent thinks 8:00 p.m. is an appropriate time for bed and the other parent insists that the child is not tired at 8:00 p.m. and should not have to go to bed until 9:00 p.m. Even if this disagreement has not happened in front of the child, a sensitive child may feel

that the parents are not in agreement and will try to use the split-and-divide approach.

The parents recognize that they need to tighten up the parental structure and plan a time to work this out between themselves. Neither parent wants to change their opinion of the bedtime, but for the child's benefit they agree to present a united parental structure and set the bedtime at 8:30 p.m. They then tell the child "we" talked about the bedtime and we have agreed that 8:30 p.m. is now the bedtime, and that each parent will now use that as the correct time.

2. Eating habits are different in different homes. If one parent is a vegetarian and the other is a meat eater, it's important that the child hears these are different views, versus that the other parent is harming the child by eating or not eating meat. The child who hears, "In this house, this is how we do it; and in the other house, that is how they do it," (without negative verbiage) can still be a healthy eater. The child who thinks they have to be concerned about what they are eating because they hear "eating meat is not good for you," or "not eating

meat is not good for you," can become anxious about what they eat and prone to develop an eating problem or disorder.

The idea that the "we" are making decisions and caring for a child can be repeated often to establish this foundational concept of how the family works. "We" will talk about this later, or "we" did have a discussion and "we" decided; these are words that help reinforce the family stability.

Single Parents:

In a single-parent home children can sometimes attempt to use the split-and-divide approach between their parents and care givers, or extended family members. If there is someone you respect as a support person, it's valuable if the children know you will confer with that person to help make a decision. A parent can share with an extended family member or caregiver their method of working with a child who will not eat lunch and wants the dessert first.

Give an example of the method and even what the parent actually does in that situation, such as: "I tell Johnny that it's my job as your parent to see that you eat well. There will be no dessert if you do not eat your lunch," or "I would like you to follow that way of working with Johnny, so he gets a consistent message and knows we are working together."

If there are major differences of how the child is cared for, a parent can always remind the child, "In this house, this is how it's done; and other people do it differently."

There is no need to give a negative connotation to how another caregiver interacts with a child. Please read the sections, for two-parent families and separated parents as they offer information that can apply to a single parent with extended family or other caregivers.

Separated Parents:

In the best circumstances, parents agree to back each other's approach on crucial issues. In some cases, a parents may not be willing to support the other parent on how to work with the child. When parents are unable to support each other, it can easily lead to the split-and-divide causing good/bad parent syndrome.

If a parent does not agree on methods used in the other parent's house, it causes the least emotional upset for the child if both parents say, "I know your mom/dad does this differently, but in my house this is what I think is the best way to do it." This is important without adding any negative slant on how the other parent is choosing to do it differently.

Please read the sections for two-parent families and single parents. They offer useful information that applies to separated parents with extended families or other caregivers.

GUIDELINE 5

The 1, 2, 3 Method

When a child learns ways to be a valued contributing member in the family, it boosts positive self-esteem and fosters a healthy atmosphere of cooperation.

Hearing positive appreciation for a child's ability to learn new ways to be (with words of encouragement), can bring about this cooperation and positive result. Saying to a child "I know you can do this," will often work in a magical way to help the child become a contributing member of the family.

There are incidents when positive words or positive reinforcements have been tried to no avail. Introducing a different approach can make a situation become a teaching opportunity for a child to learn how to be a contributing and cooperative member in the family. The *1,2,3 method* is an approach that can stop the constant need for repeating a request, set a boundary for appropriate behavior, and stop the process of continual negotiation between parent and child. It can eliminate the frustration that sometimes leads to negative communication and negative consequences.

The 1,2,3 method is most effective when the parent recognizes that the interaction with the child usually results in the child not listening to the adult when the adult has clearly stated what they need the child to do. The child may start to negotiate with the adult as if the child were an adult. Other indications when to use the 1,2,3 method are when the situation occurs often, is frustrating for both the parent and the child and is escalating rather then getting better.

When a parent decides to try the 1,2,3 method, it's best if they are able to

Saying to a child "I know you can do this," will often work in a magical way to help the child become a contributing member of the family.

follow through with it until there is resolution to a problem. Resolution can be defined as the adult asking the child to do something, i.e., pick up the toys, and the child knows this is how he or she can be cooperative, and proceeds to follow direction in an age-appropriate and timely manner.

An Example:

Here is how the 1,2, 3 method can be used in the case of a parent asking the child to clean up their toys.

A. The parent has explained to the child that they are going to try a new method to help get the toys cleaned up. The parent explains the 1,2,3 method, in an age appropriate way that the child can understand. The child clearly knows what will happen if the parent gets to #3.

B. A parent says to a child, "In a few minutes it will be time to clean up the toys." The parent can use a wind-up alarm ringer for children who need to have a concrete example of time. A parent can adjust the time to the age of a child.

When the time has elapsed the parent says, "It's now time to clean up the toys." If there are too many toys and it's overwhelming to the child, the parent can show the child a portion of the toys to be cleaned up now and the piles that can be worked on individually. The parent states clearly that they are using the 1,2,3 method and this request is #1.

C. If he child continues to play. Parent says, "That's #2, you need to clean up these toys. This is a reminder that if I have to get to #3, the consequence will be that the toys will go into the black plastic bag." The child is once again given an appropriate time frame to clean up the toys.

D. If the child ignores parent request and does not start to clean up the toys in an appropriate elapsed time frame, the parent says "That's # 3." *Then the parent gets out the black plastic bag and puts the toys in the bag.* The child has previously been apprised that if the parent gets to #3, the black bag consequence happens.

The child will often try to negotiate at this time and it's important that the parent does not engage with the negotiation. The child needs to know the consequence is reliable.

E. The child also knows that the toys can be earned back in accordance with the method that the parent has set up, i.e., "You can take three things from the black bag if you clean up the toys in a timely manner when I ask you once. If I have to remind you to clean up the toys, that counts as step two, and then you can't get anything from the black bag. If we get to step three, all the toys you have out now will go into the bag."

To work well, this system needs the following logistics in place:

- The parents involved need to agree to use the system. If this is not possible in a two-parent home, this method can still be used. The child can learn this is how one parent does clean-up and the other parent does it differently.
- The 1,2,3 method works best if not overused. It's best to use the 1,2,3 method with no more than two behaviors during any month. When those issues find resolution the method can then be transferred to other areas as needed.
- The request and consequence need to be clear and age appropriate.
- The system needs to be consistent, easily accomplished, and one that the parents using it are comfortable with doing.
- Use the 1,2,3 method when there is no choice, i.e., the toys need to be cleaned up now.

- Use a form of positive reinforcement when the child responds to a parent request at the first request. The parent says, " The toys need to be picked up." The child then proceeds to clean up the toys. This can be a positive affirmation to the child's behavior or a material reward, depending on the situation, the age of child, and the task or request that is being made.

Positive reinforcement will stabilize the new behavior to the request. "You did a great job," and "Wow, you are such a great cooperator and are contributing to a clean room." These are samples of ways to express and teach cooperation and contribution. Younger children may benefit from a simple reward system that reinforces their participation and shows parental appreciation.

Single Parents:

This method can be established in a focused manner since you can be the sole director of using the method. Being a single parent actually makes the routine of 1,2, 3 a clear, consistent approach.

If there are extended family members who regularly care for your children, or a child care worker, It's recommended that you share this method and ask for their participation in using the system you have set up. It's also important to let go of the expectation that someone outside the home will be able to duplicate what you have set up. It does not hurt to ask them to try and see if it works, since it has benefit as a conjoint effort.

Separated Parents:

Explain to the other parent the method you are using. Of course, this depends on the communication level between the parents. As noted, if separated parents do not support co-parenting, then explain to your children "In my house, this is how we do this." This is a complete statement without further explanation. It's important you do not express any negative attitudes or emotions when talking about the other parent.

GUIDELINE 6

Consistancy is Caring

Being a parent and being consistent takes many forms. There's the consistency within the routines of family life and the consistency of following through with what you say you will do. Within the reality of normal life and its normal inconsistencies, being as consistent as possible, whenever possible, is a basic guideline.

Parents often believe they can show their love and caring by listening to a child's bargaining or negotiating, and by giving in to the child's desire. Unfortunately, in situations like this, children often translate the situation as: "If you really cared for me, if I am really important to you, you would do what you say."

When any parent says something but does not do it, a child may wonder if the parent is really

43

an adult who can and will care of them. This understanding is often the hardest concept for parents to accept. Parents want the child to feel their caring. In the adult world, making changes often shows another adult that we are willing to hear their concerns and change our minds, but this behavior is confusing for a child.

The child's world is cognitively more black and white due to their limited ability for abstract thinking. There are times when negotiating and bargaining is appropriate. Winning a negotiation has a place in promoting empowered and creative children. It's appropriate to negotiate which movie to watch, what park to visit, which shirt to wear, for instance, if a parent has not made a decision, or if it does not matter to the parents.

A power struggle follows when the parent has already decided on a course of action and the child tries to move into the adult structure to manipulate a desired outcome. It's difficult to remember that when a child wins by moving into the adult structure, this can result in insecurity, and leaves the child wondering if the adult can really take care of them.

Being consistent shows your caring.

An Example:

A parent asks a child to finish a designated task before they go to visit their friend. The child does not do the assigned task. The parent really wants the child to visit their friend because they have planned to use that time for a break. The child starts negotiating and acting as another adult. Even though the child does not do what was assigned, the parent gives in and allows the child to go to the friend's house.

Unfortunately, the child often sees this as the parent not being consistent and may translate that to mean, "If my parents really cared about me, if they were really doing their job, they would follow through with what they said."

This is an example of "Don't say it if you don't want to do it," or you can't follow through with what you have started. It's also a bargaining scenario in which a child moves into an adult decision role.

> **Being consistent is a fun and easy way to express caring.**

In a situation where a parent decides that a behavior needs to have a consequence, it's not necessary to have a consequence at the moment of the incident. You can always say, "I need to think about what will be the consequence, and I will let you know by the end of the hour what I or 'we' decide." It's important to give a time frame that is appropriate to the situation and the age of a child. In a family with more then one adult involved in caretaking, you can say that you will discuss this with the other adult and figure out what the consequence will be.

Having children wait can reinforce that you really care about their well being and want to do a good job as a parent. Returning to the issue at an appropriate time will be a way to establish consistency on which the child can depend.

It's important to evaluate and accept what works for you and what does not. Remember to be realistic in your age-appropriate expectations. Be comfortable with the boundaries, rules, lifestyle and parenting environment you offer to a child. As you set up a system of consistent intent, remember that it needs to be a system you feel good about, and are able to follow through.

If you do not feel good about consistency in that particular area it will usually not last long and bring the results you desire. There is really no right or wrong system. There is just you as a unique parent individual and the unique child you are caring for. If you are a two-parent family, the systems ideally will be right for all those in the parenting group.

Another way to show consistency is giving the child a choice as often as possible, if there really is a choice. Giving a child an opportunity to make a choice (in the range of their cognitive ability) builds positive self-esteem and empowerment.

It also reinforces that when you as the parent give a child a choice, you will be consistent in letting the child do what they choose. The choice needs to be according to the children's age and their ability for abstract thinking. A child of two or three can hold the idea that they can choose between eggs and oatmeal for breakfast, if this is a real choice for that mornings breakfast. A child of two cannot hold five choices and have their decision be a clear or meaningful one.

An Example:
"Do you want eggs, oatmeal, a blueberry tart, French toast or the leftovers from last night?" In this choice, the child is overwhelmed cognitively

and chooses randomly. If you really don't care if the child has eggs or oatmeal, you can give them that choice, and they will feel that they are being heard and feel empowered in a positive way.

Being consistent can be fun and an easy way to express caring. One way to do that is to find something that you like to do with your child and incorporate that into your daily routine. Singing songs before dinner, reading a bedtime story and making breakfast together on Sundays, are just a few examples of finding ways to enjoy being consistent together.

There are many unique ways that families can incorporate rewarding, consistent routines in their daily lives. Children experience a sense of stability and feelings of well being when there are consistent routines in their daily lives.

Separated Parents:

If your separation includes visitation by both parents, be as consistent as possible in the visitation schedule. Children can adapt more easily into the transition of being in two homes if they can learn the schedule. The more consistent the schedule, the less resistant to the changes they will be and the easier it will be for the child to adjust to the changes that occur in their new environment. One way that allows a child to see consistency is making and using a calendar that shows in colors, pictures or words when the child moves from one home to another.

When a child is being dropped off at an event or a friend's house, always be clear about who is picking them up. If a child is told in a consistent manner which responsible adult is caring for them, if it is followed through, then the child can trust their parents are able to care for them even though their parents are separated.

This becomes even more important when the changeover is after school. When a child is clear about who is picking them up after school, the child can then concentrate and be present in the classroom. Learning improves.

GUIDELINE 7

Conscious Communication

In vital ways, good communication patterns are the same between adults and adults as between adults and children.

Yet In other ways, good communication skills between adults and children are very different. Children benefit from short sentence structures that have limited content. A child's consciousness is usually focused on the present moment.

Communicating about the *now* — rather than "first this," and "then that" and "after that," sentence structures — will result in far clearer communications with children. Practicing basic communication skills that are relevant for both adult-to-adult and adult-to-children teaches the children skills that will benefit them throughout their lives. It also helps adults to refine how they communicate. When you first begin to practice new communication skills, it's best to use this new method in your conversations that are not overwhelming in emotional content.

Here are four basic conscious communication practices to master:

1. **Be respectful.** Choose respectful words. Use eye contact to allow another person to know you are present and hearing what they are saying. Communication stops when one person blames, belittles or intimidates another.

2. **Take a time-out when necessary.** If unable to do step #1, let the other person know you will resume the conversation at a better time. Be clear about when you will resume the conversation.

3. **Use "I" statements only.** Speak your truth without adding "when you do ...." Any attempt to express what you are feeling that is preceded or followed with a "when you..." statement can make the other person get defensive and shut off what you are saying, for they begin to internally react and start to defend themselves.

Finding "I" statements that work may take

practice. For example, "I feel sad when I am not expressing myself clearly, and so I wonder if I am being understood." This is a good "I" statement. This is not a good "I" statement: "I am feeling sad because you are not listening to how I feel."

4. **Reflect back to what you have heard.** You want the other person to know you are really listening. You can say, "I heard you say..." and then repeat back what you heard. Be accurate and patient.

Structured Communication:

When a lot of emotional content makes it hard not to interrupt the person talking, when all else fails, use a much more structured communication process that uses five steps:

A. The first person speaks a few sentences.

B. The second person then says, "I heard you say," and repeats back what they heard. The second person then asks, "Did I miss anything?"

C. If the first person says, "You missed _____" the first person repeats back what was missed, without changing or adding anything.

D. The second person then repeats back what they had missed, "I heard you say _____."

E. This format is continued with the second person having time to share and the first person listens and says, "I heard you say _____."

This process can continue until each party feels heard and comfortable with resuming a less formal communication structure.

When the conversation is between an adult and a child, the basics can still be used with some added considerations. When talking to children, it helps to talk slowly and simply as you address one issue at a time. Remembering that children do not think like adults, the more often an adult uses good communication skills with a child, the better the outcomes of their conversations.

An Example:

The parent says, "Would you like a salad or a sandwich for lunch?" The child responds, "I want the brownies that I see on the counter."

Parent responds, " I hear that you would like the brownies for lunch, and I know how much you like them, but they are for dessert after dinner." This is an "I" statement since it acknowledges the child's feeling were heard, even without adding a "when you" statement.

Be aware that children are growing into an ability to use abstract and logical thinking and to use their reasoning skills. This awareness lets adults stay in an adult structure and helps the child be empowered to make decisions according to their cognitive ability.

When talking to children, it helps to talk slowly and simply while you address one issue at a time.

As a child's cognitive ability matures, a parent can still stay in the adult structure while setting age-appropriate choices and boundaries. As the child approaches teenage years, as cognitive ability grows toward maturity, the parent can ask for more information to make decisions, set suitable limits and allow more input to the decision-making process.

Another way to make communication between adults and children more viable is creating more common interests.

If a child loves a particular toy, it's helpful if the parent can spend time in that child's realm. This is called "floor time." It means getting down on the floor and playing Legos, dolls, cars, or just finding a creative activity that can be shared. If an adolescent watches a particular TV program that's important to them, a parent can join in watching the program. Watching the program together, playing a game together or doing any other fun activity together, creates an avenue of communication that did not exist before.

GUIDELINE 8

Create "Special Time"

Children love "special time" with each parent. Naming something as "special time" can be easy and fun for parent and child. It builds positive self-esteem for the child and helps a parent build the relationship.

"Special time" in this context means one-to-one time that you as a parent label as "our special time." The activity named as "special time" has three main components:

1. The parent has made the designation that this activity will be "special time."

2. It's one-to-one time between one parent and one child.

3. It's a time when the parent has the ability to give his/her presence and attention to the activity and the child.

It could mean a trip to the grocery store if you are creative, as long as you name it as "special time" and if the parent is able to be fully present with the child in the situation. It does not have to be something new or incredibly special so long as it has the three components.

An Example:

A grocery store "special time" would mean incorporating some of the store time with including your child's opinion on some of the items being purchased.

A parent may do this by saying, "Since we are making this grocery store trip our "special time" together, I would like you to help me decide if we should buy the ingredients for lasagna or meat loaf for dinner tonight." In this example, the parent is giving a choice that is age appropriate for the child, and the parent really does not have an attachment to the choice the child makes.

If you have more then one child in the family, "special time" with each child becomes even more valuable. Children will come to value that their parent can be fully present with them. Finding something that interests your child and joining them doing it can become "special time." It coud be a bike ride, a walk, a movie, creating art together, or gardening together.

If you have more then one child in the family "special time" with each child becomes even more valuable.

"Special time" also can be some activity created together, and with this, togetherness possibilities become endless. "Special time" may develop into a regular activity, or it can be used for different activities. "Special time" can be used to acknowledge an accomplishment, or a way to bond better during a time of challenge.

To keep "special time" alive, it should not be overused. It should always feel "special" for both of you. It can be a time to lighten up and feel your own childlike nature as you become an equal in a playful way. It's a time that is "special" to both the adult and the child. Enjoy!

Single Parents:

If a single parent has one child, it can be more difficult to separate out a "special time." They are already spending lots of one-to-one time together.

In this case, it's necessary to find an activity that is out of the daily routine and can be designated as "special time."

One option would be joining the child in doing something they already do alone in which you have not previously been involved. It could be an activity that you had previously perceived to be their alone time, or an activity that before had not interested you, but you would be willing to try. An example of this would be to sit and make a block-building time together although the child can do it without your help.

You could create a "special time" movie where you choose one you both want to see, and you can provide a "special" treat while watching it. You also could go out to photograph the neighborhood together and then create a collage together, or a set aside "special" cooking time together.

A single parent with more then one child can have difficulty creating one-to-one time with each child. This requires creativity. The benefit for the parent and the child is greater because it's so "special" to have any time set aside to be solely present with one another.

Separated Parents:

If you are separated parents who share one child, then the guidelines for single parents are the same for you.

If you are separated parents with more then one child, consider having the children separated for a visit so one-to-one time with each child can be possible. When you do have the ability to be with one child, it's still recommended that you do "special time" activity together. It will make your time together even more special.

GUIDELINE 9

The Family Is Important

Showing ways the family unit is important helps provide stability to both children and adults. As the children grow with the concept that the family is important, they have a growing understanding that their behavior and actions affect each family member. There are many ways to reinforce the concept that the family unit is an important entity within the extended family, the community and the greater world.

Like a business sets aside time to hold regular meetings of staff and employees, families benefit from holding meetings, too. Parents often make family decisions about children in an informal manner. Although this often works as a viable means in our daily life, a time set aside to discuss family issues can be very valuable for the parents and the children. The adults can find meaningful support by setting aside a time to review, revisit and plan ahead for the family meeting.

When parents set aside the time to schedule a meeting with the children, it says the family is important to them. Children directly experience that the family is important because the parents have taken time to come to a meeting with them. Children also gain a sense of active membership and a venue to voice their opinions, ideas, and complaints. This helps build their self-esteem and reinforces that everyone is an important contributing member to the family unit.

If family meetings are new to the family, use the initial meetings to develop a positive and safe environment. Initially, discuss only the "easy" issues, so that an environment of cooperation and participation is the focus, rather then trying to solve an important issue. Once the parents and children are relaxed and grasp the dynamics of the meeting, important or complex agenda items can be included as needed. Depending on the ages of the children, the agenda, the meeting length, and the issues being discussed, the family meetings can change over time.

A meeting held on a regular basis provides consistency and stresses the importance of the children's participation and membership in the family. If a family member does not come to the meeting, it's understood that person will need to accept any decisions made at the meeting they missed. If an important issue arises before the next scheduled meeting, any family member can ask to have a meeting to discuss that issue.

An Example:

1. Everyone in the family is given notice of a scheduled meeting. For older children, it can be marked on a calendar and posted so that all can remember. There's a specific time for the meeting to start and end.

2. One person is the facilitator. This can be a rotating position. Their job is guiding the meeting like an informal business meeting, helping the meeting to stay on the agenda and keeping track of the time in relation to the agenda.

3. One member is the note-taker. This can be a rotating position. Their job is writing down the agenda items and noting if an item is going to be carried over to the next meeting.

4. Each family member does a brief check-in for relating how their day went and how they feel coming to the family meeting.

5. During the meeting, no one interrupts the person talking. When a person is done expressing an issue, another member can ask a question.

6. Any member can add to the meeting agenda.

7. Everyone is given an equal opportunity to address each of the agenda items.

8. Parents can include in the agenda items that are fun and important to the children. For younger children, a relevant item could be what they would like to have for dinner.

A discussion that is age appropriate, has everyone listening without interrupting, includes even the youngest child, sets the stage for more meaningful family meetings. Examples of some agenda items are planning a vacation, reviewing the amount of screen time, allowances, household chores, and family outings.

9. Parents need to listen to the children's concerns, ideas, and opinions, and then relate that they heard the issues the children have shared. Parents do not need to make any decisions that are important to the family structure during the

meeting. They can communicate that they will take time to think about an issue, and the issue will be on the agenda for the next meeting.

10. When possible, set up the next meeting time at the close of the present meeting.

Maintaining regular family meals together is another important way to build the concept that family time is important time. Of course, there will be exceptions for meal attendance and times, but setting a dinner time or a weekend breakfast as the regular family time can be valuable to strengthen the family unit. If this cannot happen every day, set aside one or two meals that everyone will try to attend. Family members can contribute to cooking and cleaning up the meal as appropriate to ages and lifestyle.

> When children grow up with the concept that the family is important, they develop a growing understanding that their behavior and actions affect each family member.

Coming together for holidays, birthdays, graduations, and other special events can instill that it's meaningful for each family member to participate. There is an old saying, "The family that plays together stays together." Showing that families can have fun together is invaluable.

Planning an outing, a vacation or special meal together is another means of demonstrating that family time together is significant and important. Family time can be a change of routine, a family bike ride or a walk, or a vacation in which all can participate in the planning,

Demonstrating the family unit's importance is invaluable for those times when there are challenging changes or disruptions in family routines. All members become more sensitive to what it means to consider other family members in the choices they make. The family as a unit of distinctive members teaches all concerned that the family as a whole is important.

When children grow up with the concept that the family is important, they develop a growing understanding that their behavior and actions affect each family member.

Afterword

I began writing the book with these words: "Remembering the amazing miracle of life, applying the nine guidelines here with love, compassion and gratitude, can be your path to a *happy parenting, happy children* experience. The guidelines are pointers along the way; they are not rules." Please keep these words as your first and foremost guide.

I truly believe the caretakers of our children can make a positive contribution to our world. I honor and support all parents and caretakers. You are shaping the future.

Mira is available for in-person confidential sessions on Kaua'i and in northern California. She also offers worldwide phone and internet sessions. For more information or to make an appointment, contact mirasharan@pacific.net.

Thank you. Mira Walker MA/LMFT

About the Author

Mira Walker was born and raised in New York City, and she moved to California with her husband and one-year-old child in 1967. She presently has three grown sons, three daughters-in-law, and three grandchildren.

She earned a Bachelors' degree in Psychology in 1973 at San Francisco State University, and then moved to Mendocino County, California, to raise her children in a rural environment. Twelve years later at the California Institute of Integral Studies, she completed her Master's degree in Counseling Psychology with a focus on families and children. She received her Marriage Family Therapist (MFT) License in 1989.

Mira offered her services as a licensed MFT in private practice in Ukiah, California, for more than 25 years. She further was a consultant for community agencies in California. She continues to offer consultant services to active duty military families as a Military Family Life Counselor in the United States and Europe.

Resources For Parents and Helping Professionals

Child Development Institute page on Piaget (http://childdevelopmentinfo.com/child-develop ment/piaget/).

Mira Walker's website for consulting services (http://happyparentinghapppychildren.com).

The Child's Conception of the World by Jean Piaget, Joan Tomlinson (Translator), Andrew Tomlinson (Translator).

1-2-3 Magic: Effective Discipline for Children Ages 2-12 by Thomas Phelan.

How to Talk So Kids Will Listen & Listen So Kids Will Talk by Adele Faber and Elaine Mazlish.

Simplicity Parenting: Using the Extraordinary Power of Less to Raise Calmer, Happier, and More Secure Kids by Kim John Payne and Lisa M. Ross.

Parenting with Presence: Practices for Raising Conscious, Confident, Caring Kids by Susan Stiffelman, Forward by Eckhart Tolle.

Mindful Co-Parenting: A Child-Friendly Path Through Divorce by Jeremy S. Gaies, Psy.D. and Ph.D., James B. Morris, Jr.

The Single-Parent Family: Living Happily in a Changing World by Janet Spencer King.

www.ingramcontent.com/pod-product-compliance
Lightning Source LLC
Chambersburg PA
CBHW030028290326
41934CB00005B/528